HOT

Celebrity Biographies

Daniel Radcliffe

FILM AND STAGE STAR

STEPHANIE WATSON

Enslow Publishers, Inc.
40 Industrial Road
Box 398
Berkeley Heights, NJ 07922
USA
http://www.enslow.com

Library of Congress Cataloging-in-Publication Data
Watson, Stephanie, 1969-
  Daniel Radcliffe : film and stage star / by Stephanie Watson.
      p. cm. – (Hot celebrity biographies)
  Includes bibliographical references and index.
  Summary: "Find out how Daniel became Harry Potter, his likes, dislikes, and what he does with his free time"–Provided by publisher.
  ISBN-13: 978-0-7660-3209-5
  ISBN-10: 0-7660-3209-4
  1. Radcliffe, Daniel, 1989–Juvenile literature. 2. Actors–Great Britain–Biography–Juvenile literature. I. Title.
  PN2598.R27W38 2009
  791.4302'8092–dc22
  [B]
                                    2008026470

Paperback ISBN-13: 978-0-7660-3209-5
Paperback ISBN-10: 0-7660-3624-6

Printed in the United States of America

10 9 8 7 6 5 4 3 2 1

Photographs: Niviere/Sipa/AP Images, 1; Anthony Harvey/AP Images, 4, 38; Murray Close/Warner Bros./AP Images, 7, 27, 29; Matt Sayles/AP Images, 8, 26; Adam Butler/AP Images, 11, 19; Dave Caulkin/AP Images, 12, 14; Remy de la Mauviniere/AP Images, 17; Alastair Grant/AP Images, 18; Shuji Kajiyama/AP Images, 22; Diane Bondareff/AP Images, 25; Tammie Arroyo/AP Images, 30; Jim Cooper/AP Images, 32; Jennifer Graylock/AP Images, 33; Richard Drew/AP Images, 35; Paul Drinkwater/NBCU Photo Bank/AP Images, 37; Mark J. Terrill/AP Images, 41; Jason DeCrow/AP Images, 43

Cover photo: Daniel Radcliffe attends the Orange British Academy Film Awards in 2008. Niviere/Sipa/AP Images.

Contents

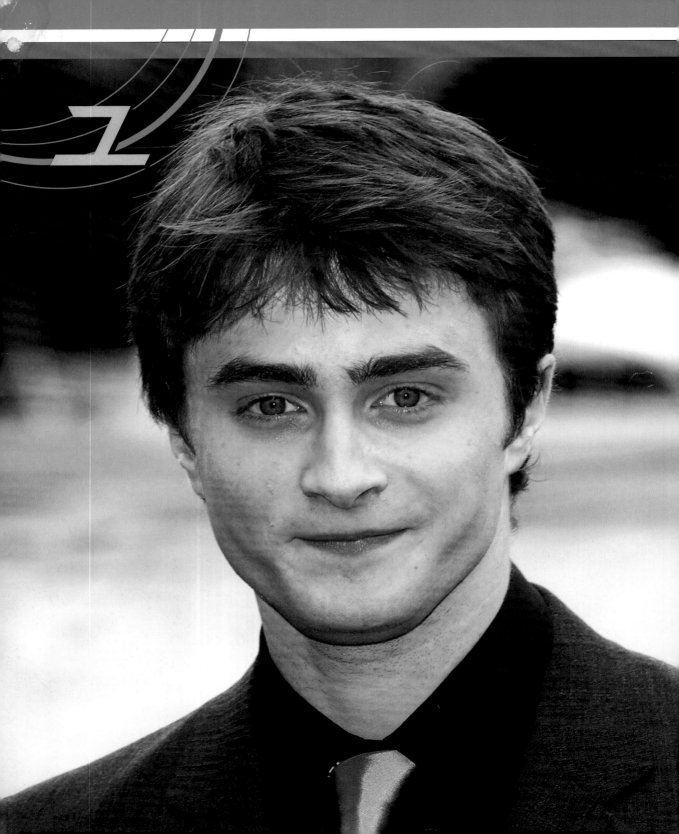

▲ *Daniel Radcliffe is shown in a scene from* Harry Potter and the Order of the Phoenix.

series *Inspector Lynley Mysteries* and the movie *The Government Inspector*. Both Alan and Marcia work in the entertainment industry, and their son soon followed in their footsteps.

SCHOOL DAYS

In 1997, the first Harry Potter book was released in the United Kingdom. Its main character attended Hogwarts School of Witchcraft and Wizardry, a school for wizards and witches. The school could only be reached by boarding a train through a secret platform—platform nine and

7

▲ *Daniel Radcliffe signs autographs on his way to a premiere.*

three-quarters—at King's Cross Station in London. Students at the school took classes such as Herbology, the History of Magic, and Defense Against the Dark Arts.

Daniel attended an all-boys school called Sussex House in Chelsea, a town about a mile away from his home. It is a private school, but in England, private schools are actually called "public schools." The schools are privately owned and charge tuition. Daniel's favorite classes were gym and science. While in school, Daniel started to take an interest in acting and began getting parts in plays.

A BUDDING ACTOR

Those first parts were far from glamorous, though. "My earliest memory of acting was playing a monkey in a school play, when I was about six. I had floppy ears and orange makeup, and I had to wear tights," he told *E! Online* in 2001. "I hope nobody ever digs up a picture of me in that, because it was embarrassing." Much bigger and better roles were to come in the future.

Daniel was lucky that both his parents had connections. Many of their friends had important jobs in television, theater, and film. Some of these friends got to know the budding actor. They thought he had real potential. When Daniel was about ten years old, one family friend thought he might be perfect for a TV movie called *Oliver Twist*. The movie was based on the book by Charles Dickens. It was the story of an orphan who becomes a pickpocket to survive on the streets of London.

Although it would have been a big break for Daniel, his parents weren't convinced. They were afraid to let their son act on television and possibly become famous. They just wanted him to be a normal kid.

Daniel's parents finally gave in because they could tell their son needed a confidence boost. Daniel has a mild brain disorder called dyspraxia. The condition can make a person seem clumsy. It also can affect a person's normal process of learning. Because of his dyspraxia, Daniel struggled at school. When he started acting, he finally found his strength.

DAVID COPPERFIELD

A TV movie based on another one of Charles Dickens's books, *David Copperfield*, was being cast. Daniel again caught the attention of a family friend in the industry. Daniel tried out for the role of the young David Copperfield. After five tryouts, he got the part in 1999.

Daniel shared the screen with some of the biggest names in English film. Dame Maggie Smith played Aunt Betsey. (Daniel worked with her again a few years later, when she donned Professor McGonagall's crooked witch's hat in the Harry Potter films.) Sir Ian McKellen played the nasty headmaster, Mr. Creakle. And Bob Hoskins played Wilkins Micawber, a man who was always in debt.

David Copperfield premiered on the BBC television network in England on Christmas Day, 1999. It also aired as part of the *Masterpiece Theatre* series on the PBS network in the United States. Reviewers couldn't get enough of the young actor. The *Christian Science Monitor* called Daniel ". . . real as rain. Those wonderful eyes and cherubic face make us feel every thorn and every joy with equal truth."

His acting career was just taking off with *David Copperfield*. But, Daniel did what most actors put off doing until they have been in the business for many years. He took a break and went back to school. The break wouldn't last long,

▲ *Radcliffe is pictured with a chess piece used in the first Harry Potter movie.*

though. By the following year, Daniel already had landed another role. This time he was acting in a major feature film called *The Tailor of Panama*. It was about a spy who travels to Panama and gets caught up with a tailor who is linked to gangsters.

Daniel played Mark Pendel, the son of the tailor in the movie's title. Though Daniel had a small part, it was a big-budget, high-profile movie. What he didn't know at the time was that an even bigger movie was headed his way.

Becoming "Harry Potter"

In 1997, an English film producer named David Heyman was looking for a children's book to turn into a movie. An assistant brought him the book *Harry Potter and the Sorcerer's Stone* to read. He'd never heard of it. But after reading the book, Heyman knew he'd found his movie.

Heyman got permission from J. K. Rowling to turn her book into a film. He pulled together a budget of $125 million to make the movie. And he hired Chris Columbus to direct it.

Heyman had his story, and his plans were coming together. There was only one thing missing—Harry Potter. It was two months before the movie was supposed to start shooting. He still couldn't find the right actor to play the young wizard.

Heyman and Columbus wanted to find an actor who not only looked like the character Rowling had described—the boy with the "thin face, knobbly knees, black hair, and bright green eyes." They also wanted someone who could capture

◄ *Daniel Radcliffe was picked to play "Harry Potter" in 2000. He was eleven years old.*

▲ *Director Chris Columbus* (right) *finally found the right "Harry Potter."*

Harry's spirit. They were searching for "an old soul in a child's body," said Heyman.

The search for someone to play Harry Potter was a huge effort that cost millions of dollars. One famous actor after another was turned down. At one point Heyman thought about casting American actor Haley Joel Osment. Osment had been nominated for an Oscar award for his work in *The Sixth Sense*. Still, Heyman didn't think he was right for the part of Harry. Someone even suggested that Harry Potter be computer animated so they wouldn't have to find an actor to play him. Yet Heyman finally decided that the actor who played Harry should be British and unknown. Most important, he would be real—not animated.

As time passed, Heyman and Columbus both started to get nervous.

They auditioned thousands of young actors. The thought of becoming Harry Potter drew huge crowds of hopefuls. At one audition in England, 40,000 boys showed up. Radcliffe wasn't among them, though. Later he told the *Detroit Free Press* he was "dead keen" on becoming Harry Potter. That was his way of saying that he really wanted to do it. Still, his parents were afraid that he'd be too disappointed if he didn't get the part. So he didn't try out.

Then one night, Radcliffe and his parents were at the theater seeing a comedy play called *Stones in His Pockets.* During the play, Radcliffe became aware that the two men sitting in front of him kept turning around to stare at him. He thought it was strange at first. Then he found out that the men were David Heyman and a screenwriter named Steve Kloves. For Heyman and Kloves, that chance meeting was the discovery they had been waiting for. As Heyman told the *Detroit Free Press*, "Right then, I knew I had found our Harry."

SCREEN TEST

Unlike many of his friends, Radcliffe wasn't a huge fan of the Harry Potter books. But he knew a good opportunity when he saw one.

When David Heyman and Steve Kloves invited him to the film studio for lunch, he jumped at the chance. During the visit, Radcliffe got to watch as the crew built the set for Hogwarts. He took three screen tests to see how well he might fit into the role of Harry Potter. In one of the scenes he played opposite Hagrid, the giant groundskeeper who befriends Harry, Ron, and Hermione. Robbie Coltrane, the actor who plays Hagrid, kept "fumbling the lines . . . to see what I would do," Radcliffe told *Masterpiece Theatre Online*. Radcliffe had to improvise to keep up. In another of his screen tests, Radcliffe had to pretend that he was riding a broomstick.

The day after his third screen test, Radcliffe was taking a bath when his father gave him the good news. He had gotten the part of Harry Potter. "I was so happy, I cried," Radcliffe told the *Christian Science Monitor*. He was so excited that he could barely sleep that night. He woke up at 2:30 A.M. and went into his parents' bedroom so they could tell him that he hadn't been dreaming. Radcliffe was just eleven years old. He was about to play one of the most famous characters in recent history.

When Rowling heard that Radcliffe had gotten the part, she thought he was the perfect choice. After meeting him, she told producer David Heyman, "I feel like I've been reunited with my long-lost son."

HOW MUCH LIKE "HARRY POTTER" IS DANIEL RADCLIFFE?

Many actors don't like being compared to the characters they play. But Radcliffe has been very honest about his similarities to "Harry Potter." In fact, he joked at a 2002 press conference that he has so much in common with his character that he's probably "going to have to have therapy one day."

Both Harry Potter and Daniel Radcliffe are intense, serious, curious, and loyal. Neither is afraid to stand up for himself or his friends, even if it means getting into trouble.

Radcliffe found it very easy to find the similarities with his character because J. K. Rowling had described Harry Potter so clearly in her books. "What I love about playing Harry is that he's a really real character . . . complicated, but he's very accessible," he said while on *The Early Show*.

The one thing the two boys definitely don't share, however, is magic. If he could have any of Harry's powers, Radcliffe has said he'd choose the invisibility cloak. "To move about without anyone seeing you, that would be brilliant," he told the *Detroit Free Press* in 2001.

▶ *Two fans show off their "Harry Potter" costumes.*

▲ *"Harry Potter" made Radcliffe an overnight celebrity.*

On August 21, 2000, the Warner Brothers movie studio made the big announcement: Daniel Radcliffe was going to star in *Harry Potter and the Sorcerer's Stone*. Radcliffe's friends were quick to call and congratulate him when they heard the news. They were all happy for him. "None of them—not one single person—was jealous," Radcliffe told *PBS Online*.

HARRY POTTER SHOOTS— AND SCORES

Harry Potter and the Sorcerer's Stone was filmed at Leavesden Studios, a former airplane factory about 20 miles outside of London. It was the same studio in which director George Lucas had filmed *Star Wars: Episode II—Attack of the Clones*.

On the first day of shooting, Radcliffe was terrified that he would "muck it up completely," he told CNN in 2001. He couldn't afford to mess up—the producer, director, cast, and 1,600 crew members were all counting on him.

During the shoot, Radcliffe had to be on set for four hours a day (under British law that was the highest number of hours a child under the age of sixteen could work). While filming, he missed several months of school. He studied with a private tutor on the set.

Life on the set of *Harry Potter and the Sorcerer's Stone* wasn't all hard work, though. The cast and crew still had time for fun. Radcliffe and his costars Emma Watson (who played Hermione Granger) and Rupert Grint (cast as Ron Weasley)

▼ *Daniel Radcliffe* (center) *is pictured with the rest of the cast of* Harry Potter and the Sorcerer's Stone *in 2001.*

DID YOU KNOW?

Daniel Radcliffe tried to read the first Harry Potter book when he was eight years old, but he didn't finish it. He didn't read the entire book until he was cast in the movie.

all loved playing practical jokes on one another and the crew. One day, Watson and Grint put signs reading "kick me" and "pull my hair" all over Radcliffe's back. "And he'd walk around for like ten minutes without noticing," Watson told *The Today Show*. Another time, Radcliffe programmed everyone's cell phones into different languages. He made Robbie Coltrane's phone speak Turkish.

HARRY POTTER PREMIERES

The film took eleven months of shooting and many months of editing. Finally, *Harry Potter and the Sorcerer's Stone* opened in theaters on November 16, 2001. To promote the movie, Warner Brothers launched one of the biggest publicity campaigns in history. The studio hung posters featuring Radcliffe all over London, Manhattan, and other big cities.

Although Radcliffe didn't mind the attention, he admitted that he was nervous at the movie premiere in London. "I hate watching myself. I really, really hate it," he told CNN.

With more than 10,000 fans on hand, the opening was scary for the young star. Radcliffe had no reason to be worried. He was a huge hit as Harry Potter. "Dan nailed it. And I am very pleased," J. K. Rowling said, according to a statement in the *Toronto Star*. "Dan was so instinctive, and so right," Richard Harris told *BBC Online*. Harris played Professor Dumbledore until the actor died in 2002.

Harry Potter and the Sorcerer's Stone was a major hit. It earned close to $1 billion. For his work on the film, Radcliffe won the Variety Club of Great Britain's Best Newcomer Award and the David di Donatello Award. The David is a major movie award in Italy. Radcliffe became so popular an actor that his father, Alan, quit his job to become his full-time chaperone. Radcliffe had six more Harry Potter movies and several other acting projects ahead of him. He would need the extra help.

"Harry Potter," Take Two

Radcliffe barely had time to take a breath after *Harry Potter and the Sorcerer's Stone*. Shooting on the second film in the series, *Harry Potter and the Chamber of Secrets*, began almost immediately after the first movie wrapped.

Filming the story of Harry Potter's second year at Hogwarts was even more challenging than the first movie had been. In one scene, Radcliffe had to battle an 80-foot serpent called a basilisk in the Chamber of Secrets. "It was hard to fight. I kept knocking its teeth out," he told the *Toronto Sun*. The crew had to keep repairing the basilisk prop and shoot the scene over and over again.

In other scenes, Radcliffe had to act opposite an orange ball. It was a stand-in for the house elf, Dobby. Computers later were used to fill in the animated character. Radcliffe had to use all his acting talents to make the scene look real. He had to make sure that his eyes were even with the ball so it looked like he was actually looking at Dobby.

◀ *Daniel Radcliffe answers reporters' questions about the second Harry Potter movie.*

Radcliffe and his costars had to be on set for nine hours each day. That included three hours of schoolwork and one hour for lunch. He also had to go through one of the biggest changes in life in front of millions of movie viewers— puberty. As often happens as boys get older, Radcliffe's voice began to crack. Luckily, Harry also was at an age when his voice normally would break, so no one seemed to notice.

Harry Potter and the Chamber of Secrets hit the theaters in November 2002. It became the top-grossing movie of that year, earning $866 million. Radcliffe's star just kept rising.

POTTER MANIA

The next movie, *Harry Potter and the Prisoner of Azkaban*, began production on February 21, 2003. It had a new director, Mexican filmmaker Alfonso Cuarón. His first task for the three young stars was a homework assignment. They each had to write an essay about their character. Just as Hermione would have done, Watson wrote a thorough eleven-page report. In true Ron Weasley form, Grint never handed in his paper. And like his character, Radcliffe wrote a short one-page summary.

Every Harry Potter movie has featured some of the best-known actors in film, and this one was no different. Gary Oldman came on board to play Harry Potter's godfather,

Sirius Black. Oldman already had starred in dozens of movies. He often played the bad guy. In the Harry Potter movies, he was the good guy for a change.

Radcliffe was thrilled to be acting with Oldman, who was one of his heroes. The two became friends during filming. When Gary found out that Radcliffe loved music, he bought him a bass guitar and some lessons as a gift.

Harry Potter and the Prisoner of Azkaban premiered in the summer of 2004. At the same time, filming on the next movie, *Harry Potter and the Goblet of Fire*, began. The plot focused on the Triwizard Tournament, a competition between

▼ *Daniel Radcliffe, Rupert Grint, and Emma Watson act in a scene from* Harry Potter and the Order of the Phoenix, *the fifth installment.*

▲ Harry Potter and the Order of the Phoenix *was released in 2007.*

Hogwarts and two other wizardry schools. It was darker and more emotional than the other Harry Potter films had been.

Near the end of the movie, Harry loses a classmate and must tell the boy's father that his son has died. "I had to tap into emotions that I personally never felt," he told *USA Today* in 2005.

Radcliffe also had to shoot some of the trickiest scenes of his career. One was a tournament challenge that takes place completely underwater. He spent six months training for the scene. It was shot in a 20-foot-deep tank. Director Mike Newell and the actors had to "talk" to one another using hand signs because they couldn't open their mouths underwater.

Radcliffe did have to keep his eyes open underwater during the scene. That meant that they couldn't shoot more than fifteen seconds of the scene at a time. His eyes stung, and he kept getting ear infections. Still, Radcliffe insisted on doing the scene without a stunt double.

The underwater scene seemed easy compared to other scenes he had to shoot. "The worst was the dragon sequence, where I fall down the roof," he told *Rolling Stone* in 2005. In the scene, he had to slide down a 50-foot roof while attached to a thin wire. "It was terrifying. I don't have a problem with heights. It's just falling from them that I'm not so keen on," he said.

The whole shoot was difficult. Radcliffe spent long days on the movie set. On an average day, the studio car would pick him up at 7:30 in the morning. He wouldn't get home until around 7:30 at night.

THE DEATHLY HALLOWS

Harry Potter and the Half-Blood Prince was filmed in 2007. That was the same year in which the

▶ *Daniel Radcliffe* (center) *has fun with his costars.*

final book in the series, *Harry Potter and the Deathly Hallows*, came out in bookstores. Its release was a major event for Harry Potter fans. Everyone wanted to know how the story ended.

Even though he played Harry on screen, Radcliffe didn't get a sneak peak at the book. He had to wait for it to be released, just like everyone else. When *People* magazine asked Radcliffe whether he thought his character might die, he said, "I think I will. I sort of hope I will, really. . . . I'm quite looking forward to doing a death scene, if I get that opportunity." Radcliffe finally learned the fate of his character when he read the book on July 22, 2007. It was the day after the book had come out and just one day before Radcliffe's eighteenth birthday.

The idea of filming the last Harry Potter movie was bittersweet for Radcliffe. "It's absolutely the end of an era," he told *USA Today* in 2007. At the same time, he felt as though he'd been playing Harry for long enough. Radcliffe told *People* magazine that he's "the only kid in the world who doesn't want an eighth Harry Potter book." The next chapter in Radcliffe's life was waiting to be written.

FIRST KISS

With seven different Harry Potter movies to film, Radcliffe had to grow up in front of the camera. He got taller, his voice changed, and stubble started to pop up on his face. As Radcliffe grew up, so did his character. In the fifth movie, *Harry Potter and the Order of the Phoenix*, it was time for Harry to have his first kiss.

To audiences, Harry's kiss with Cho Chang (played by Katie Leung) was major news. To Radcliffe, though, it wasn't as earth shattering. He already had kissed a girl for a movie called *December Boys*. Although he was a bit nervous to be kissing a girl in front of the huge Harry Potter cast and crew, it was just like filming any other scene.

The kiss with Cho Chang wouldn't be Radcliffe's last on-screen kiss either. In *Harry Potter and the Half-Blood Prince*, his character begins dating Ron's sister, Ginny Weasley (played by actress Bonnie Wright). Because Radcliffe had known Wright since she was ten years old, he said it felt very odd to be kissing her.

▶ *Fans have seen Daniel Radcliffe grow up on screen.*

Fame and Fortune

The Harry Potter movies turned Radcliffe from a normal teenager into a huge star. A wax figure of him was created at Madame Tussaud's Museum in London. He had an imprint made of his hands, feet, and Harry's famous wand in the sidewalk outside of Mann's Chinese Theater in Hollywood.

He went to parties and premieres and met big stars such as Ben Stiller, Tim Robbins, and Susan Sarandon.

With stardom came girls—lots of them. Their interest in Radcliffe started when he was still very young. "When I was about twelve, I was walking down the street next to this girl in France, and she started screaming! And I was really frightened, so I started screaming," he told *Rolling Stone* in 2005.

One day, Radcliffe was riding in a limo in New York. It pulled up to a stoplight. A car pulled up next to them. Suddenly, a girl leaned out the car window and tried to climb into the window of Radcliffe's car. She hung over the street, half in her car and half in Radcliffe's limo. Radcliffe and the other passengers screamed for her to get back in her car. Luckily, the girl wasn't hurt.

Fans followed Radcliffe everywhere—even home. At his parents' house in England, the doorbell would ring almost every afternoon. It was always a different girl asking the same question: "Does Daniel live here?"

"The fans know our address, the names of the dogs, the color of the walls," Radcliffe's mother, Marcia, told the British newspaper, the *Sunday Times*. Although she did tell the fans

▲ *Daniel Radcliffe and Emma Watson have never dated, but they are good friends.*

that Radcliffe lived there, she said it "in a tone that will make them never, ever come back."

LOVE LIFE

Everyone knows that girls like Radcliffe. Naturally, people have wondered which girls he likes. At first, people thought he might be dating his Harry Potter costar, Emma Watson. He says that they've never dated. In fact, he thinks of her almost like a sister. "But I had a big crush on her when I first met her, definitely," he told *TIME* magazine in 2005.

Radcliffe has had serious girlfriends in the past, and he does want a relationship. One thing that he has said, though, is that he prefers not to date actresses.

BRITAIN'S RICHEST TEEN

Along with fame came fortune. When Radcliffe made the first Harry Potter movie, he earned about $320,000. That's a lot more than the few dollars most kids earn on a paper route or babysitting. By Hollywood standards, though, it wasn't very much money.

By the time he made the fifth movie, *Harry Potter and the Order of the Phoenix*, Radcliffe had gotten a big raise. He was paid $14 million for that film. By 2005 he had earned enough money to be named Britain's richest teen. When he turned eighteen two years later, Radcliffe was worth about $35 million.

Even more money was to come. In 2007, Radcliffe signed a deal to make the last two Harry Potter movies. He would earn a total of $50 million for the movies.

Radcliffe was rich— very rich. When his career was first taking

▶ *Daniel Radcliffe greets his fans.*

off, his parents decided that he needed to take very good care of that money so he still would have it when he grew up. Just a month after Radcliffe landed the first Harry Potter role, they set up a company called Gilmore Jacobs to manage his money.

Radcliffe's parents know that their son earns more money than they do. But they don't seem to mind. "We just joke about it, to be honest," Radcliffe told an Australian newspaper, the *Herald Sun*, in 2007. "They don't think of me as the bread-earner of the family."

Radcliffe has millions of dollars in the bank. Still, you'll probably never see him buying a huge mansion in Hollywood. He has never liked displays of wealth. His tastes are much more modest. "The things I like buying are things that cost about ten dollars—books and CDs and DVDs," he told the *New York Times*. Although he's grateful to have the money, Radcliffe says it's not what makes him want to be an actor.

SUCCESS HASN'T SPOILED HIM

Radcliffe may have millions of dollars in the bank and his picture in every teen magazine. But he's never let success spoil him.

NEW YORK APARTMENT

Even as he has earned millions of dollars from the Harry Potter movies, Radcliffe has lived in the same small room in his parents' London home. He did spend money on one piece of real estate, however.

In December 2007, he bought a $4.3 million apartment on Mercer Street in New York. The apartment was designed by famous architect Jean Nouvel. It is in the trendy SoHo neighborhood.

The apartment has two bedrooms, two-and-a-half bathrooms, and windows that reach from the floor to the ceiling. In the building are a pool, steam room, and concierge.

Even though he bought an amazing apartment, Radcliffe hasn't lived in it. Right after he bought the apartment, his parents' company, Gilmore Jacobs, made it available to rent for a cost of $20,000 a month.

▲ Daniel Radcliffe arrives at a premiere in 2007.

"I go out with my friends. I go to the cinema—all the normal things that teenagers do," he said on the Warner Brothers Harry Potter Web site. He says his friends still treat him the same way they did before he became famous.

Despite all of his money and fame, Radcliffe isn't the typical teen actor. You're not likely to see him speeding down the road in a flashy sports car while being chased by photographers. He doesn't go out with a different young woman every night, as some actors do. He stays away from drugs and alcohol. In fact, Radcliffe is pretty boring as celebrities go.

Everyone who works with and knows Radcliffe says what a nice guy he is. "He still thanks me after each take," director Chris Columbus told the *Chicago Sun-Times*.

Radcliffe has such a "nice guy" image that one television show made fun of him for it. When he was a guest on the HBO series *Extras* in 2006, Radcliffe played a real brat. His character was a nasty version of himself. The character swore, smoked cigarettes, and tried to date an older woman. "I had a real laugh doing it," he told the *Herald Sun*.

Life after "Harry Potter"

After you've played the world's most famous wizard, where do you go next? It's easy for an actor who has played such a popular role to be connected to his character forever. This is called "typecasting." It makes it difficult for the actor to get

▲ *Now that the Harry Potter movies are wrapping up, Daniel Radcliffe is looking to the future.*

other types of parts. Radcliffe knew people thought of him as Harry Potter. That's why he started planning for his future long before the end of the movie series.

In 2005, between shooting the fourth and fifth Harry Potter movies, Radcliffe decided to do a very different kind of film. The movie was called *December Boys*.

▲ *Radcliffe has moved on to more adult roles, such as his role in* December Boys.

Radcliffe's character was as far from Harry Potter as he could get. "I needed just to prove to myself that I could absolutely go off and do something else," he told *Entertainment Weekly*. The movie was based on a book by Michael Noonan. The story takes place in the 1960s. It follows four orphans as they go on a summer vacation by the ocean. Radcliffe traveled to Adelaide and Kangaroo Island in Australia to shoot the film. He played the oldest orphan, named Maps. For the role he picked up a very real-sounding Australian accent.

The movie showed people that Radcliffe could play a character other than Harry Potter. Roger Ebert, a film critic with the *Chicago Sun-Times,* wrote, "Radcliffe is convincing as the young man; he proves he can move beyond the Harry role."

DANIEL GROWS UP

If he really wanted to escape from the part of Harry Potter, Radcliffe's next role was sure to help. In 2007, when he was seventeen, he spent four months starring in the play *Equus* in London's West End theater district. In the show, Radcliffe played a young man named Alan Strang.

Many people were surprised that Radcliffe took the part because the play had very adult themes. Radcliffe's character is disturbed. He blinds horses. He also appears on stage without his clothing.

Radcliffe has said that he wasn't trying to separate himself from Harry Potter by playing Alan Strang. He was just trying to take many different types of roles. Radcliffe also hoped

A GOOD DEED

Many actors use their wealth and fame to help charities. Radcliffe is no exception. In 2008, he donated a gray, metal-framed pair of glasses to an exhibit remembering victims of the Holocaust. During the Holocaust in the 1930s and 1940s, the Nazis killed six million Jews in Europe. Radcliffe's mother is Jewish.

With his glasses, Radcliffe included a note that read: "Please find enclosed my first pair of glasses which I wore at school at six. I wish you every success with the exhibition."

Glasses donated by celebrities and others were linked together in the shape of a train track. Trains carrried many of the Nazis' victims to concentration camps. Later the glasses were auctioned for charity.

that he could get Harry Potter fans who didn't normally go to the theater to see his show.

J. K. Rowling came to see the show one night. She loved it, and she and Radcliffe had dinner together afterward. The producer of the play, David Pugh, thought Radcliffe did a great job in the part. "He had incredible presence and was very professional," he told *Variety* in 2007.

The fans loved *Equus* too. Hordes of them showed up at the stage door every night, trying to get in. The paparazzi also crowded the stage door each night. They were trying to snap pictures of Radcliffe to sell to magazines. To annoy them, Radcliffe

▲ *Daniel Radcliffe donated this pair of glasses to an exhibition marking National Holocaust Memorial Day in 2008.*

would wear the same jacket and hat every single night. "So they could take photos for six months, but it would look like the same day," he told Jay Leno on *The Tonight Show*.

WHAT DOES THE FUTURE HOLD?

Harry Potter and the Deathly Hallows is the final movie in the Harry Potter series. It was set to be released in 2010. After playing the same famous character for ten years, what comes next for Radcliffe? He has said that he hopes to keep acting.

41

As he was working on the last of the seven movies in the series, Radcliffe already had his eye on the future and life after Harry Potter. He signed up to act in the play *Equus* again, this time on Broadway in New York. Radcliffe was hoping that the dark character in *Equus* would help him shed his boy-wizard image.

Radcliffe also agreed to star in the film *Journey*. The movie is based on the diaries of Dan Eldon. Eldon was a photographer who was killed in Mogadishu, a city in the east African country of Somalia. Eldon's family thought Radcliffe would be perfect for the role. "He has a sense of humor and energy inside him which reminds me of Dan," Eldon's mother, Kathy, told the *Herald Sun.*

Beyond these roles, there's no way to know what the future holds for Daniel Radcliffe. In real life, he has no powers to help him see what twists and turns his career will take. However, people close to him predict a very magical future. "He has an incredible work ethic, and he's determined to push himself as an actor," David Yates, director of *Order of the Phoenix*, told *USA Today.* "I just think he's going to get better and better."

Daniel Radcliffe appears onstage during ▶
MTV's Total Request Live *in 2007.*

Timeline

1989 Daniel Radcliffe is born on July 23

1999 Appears in *David Copperfield* on the BBC television network

2000 Chosen to play "Harry Potter"

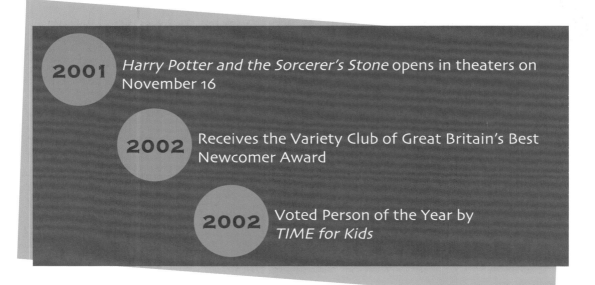

2001 *Harry Potter and the Sorcerer's Stone* opens in theaters on November 16

2002 Receives the Variety Club of Great Britain's Best Newcomer Award

2002 Voted Person of the Year by *TIME for Kids*

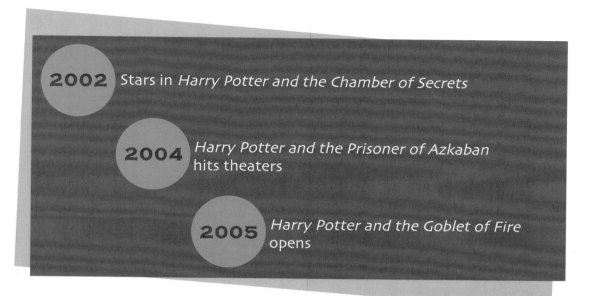

2002 Stars in *Harry Potter and the Chamber of Secrets*

2004 *Harry Potter and the Prisoner of Azkaban* hits theaters

2005 *Harry Potter and the Goblet of Fire* opens

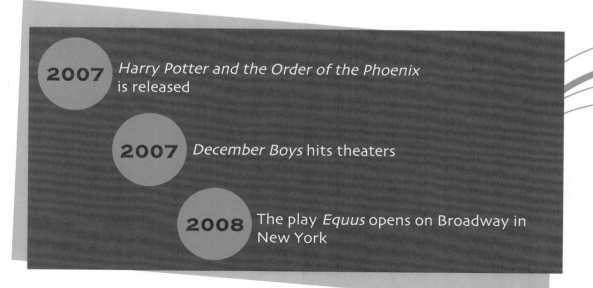

2007 *Harry Potter and the Order of the Phoenix* is released

2007 *December Boys* hits theaters

2008 The play *Equus* opens on Broadway in New York

Further Info

Books

Beahm, George W. *Muggles and Magic: An Unofficial Guide to J. K. Rowling and the Harry Potter Phenomenon.* Charlottesville, VA: Hampton Roads, 2007.

Kieve, Paul. *Hocus Pocus.* New York: Scholastic, Inc., 2008. (Introduction by Daniel Radcliffe)

Norwich, Grace. *Daniel Radcliffe: No Ordinary Wizard.* New York: Simon Spotlight, 2005.

DVDs

David Copperfield (2000). Dir. Simon Curtis. BBC Warner, 2006.

Harry Potter and the Sorcerer's Stone: Special Widescreen Edition (2001). Dir. Chris Columbus. Warner Home Video, 2002.

Internet Addresses

Daniel Radcliffe
http://www.danradcliffe.co.uk/

DanRadcliffe.com
http://www.danradcliffe.com

Harry Potter, Scholastic Kids
http://www.scholastic.com/harrypotter/

Glossary

agent—Someone who helps authors get their books published or helps actors find roles.

basilisk—A giant deadly snake that was kept beneath Hogwarts School of Witchcraft and Wizardry in *Harry Potter and the Chamber of Secrets.*

casting director—A person who finds actors to fill roles in movies and TV shows.

chaperone—An adult who travels with and protects the safety of a young girl or boy.

cherubic—Sweet and angel-like.

concierge—A person who works for a hotel or apartment building. He or she makes dinner reservations and helps guests and residents with other requests.

paparazzi—A photographer who takes pictures of celebrities.

pickpocket—Someone who steals money or other items from people's pockets or purses.

typecast—Cast again and again in the same type of movie, television, or theater role.

Index